ENTREPRENEUR'S ROAD MAP:
10 KEY STEPS FOR PREPARING YOUR BUSINESS PLAN

Delroy V. Morgan

ENTREPRENEUR'S ROAD MAP

Copyright © 2024 by Delroy V. Morgan
All rights reserved.
Published by:
Zing4Success Strategic Management and Planning LLC
Website: https://zing4success.com
Email: Delroy.Morgan@zing4success.com

The content in this book belongs to Delroy V. Morgan. All rights reserved. No part of this book may be reproduced, distributed, or transmitted in any form or by any means including photocopying, recording, or other electronic or mechanical methods without the prior written permission of the publisher. Copying this book is illegal.

ISBN: 979-8-9893021-1-6

Library of Congress Control Number 204900117

ENTREPRENEUR'S ROAD MAP

Who should read this book?

If you are a business owner, an entrepreneur or a business plan preparer and you want to know the information to include in a business plan you should find this book invaluable. Some readers may have attended one of Zing4Success Strategic Management and Planning's seminars or webinars and you need reminders or additional guidelines, this book is also for you. The author has organized the book in 10 distinct sections, complete with illustrations so that you can follow along as you prepare your business plan.

ENTREPRENEUR'S ROAD MAP

Acknowledgements

It is a pleasure to acknowledge and express my sincere gratitude to all the individuals who supported my efforts to bring this book to you. Thanks to my wife, Mary L. Morgan, for her feedback, cover photograph and encouragement, and to my children, Rashida Morgan-Brown, and Omari Morgan, for their thoughtful inputs. I am grateful to Dr. Mark Headley for his proofreading skills and assistance in title selection as well as ideas for cover designs. Thanks to Steve O. Johnson for his help in proofreading and his excellent suggestions. I am also thankful to Grace White for her copyediting expertise and to Rashida Morgan-Brown for her insight and creative expertise in the final overall cover designs.

Your valuable inputs have made it possible to hone the information in this book to be more comprehensive and relevant for our readers.

Table of Contents

Introduction and Overview 1
    What is a business plan? 1
    How do I start? 2
    Why do I need to write a business plan? 3
    How should a business plan be used? 3
    What are the steps after writing the business plan? 4
STEP 1 – Prepare an Executive Summary 6
    Synopsis of Management Expectations 6
    Purpose, Goals, Mission and Vision 6
STEP 2 – Share Your Company Description 14
    Type of Business and Structure 14
    Expertise and Strength 14
    Organization History 14
STEP 3 – Outline Market Strategy and Analysis 20
    Demographics 20
    Target Market 21
    Pricing 21
    Research and Surveys 21
    Competitive Analysis Including SWOT 24
    Market Share 27
    Added Value and Competitive Advantage 28
STEP 4 – Describe Your Products and Services 31
    Value and Benefits 31

ENTREPRENEUR'S ROAD MAP

STEP 5 – Discuss Marketing and Sales Plan 35
    Website and Videos 35
    Promotions 35
    Collaboration 36
    Sales Projections 36

STEP 6 – Provide an Overview of Operations Plan 40
    Shipping 40
    Damaged Goods 41
    Inventory 41
    Suppliers/Payments 41
    Credit Policy 42

STEP 7 – Present a Management Plan 45
    Leadership Team 45
    Structure 45
    Compensation 47

STEP 8 – Develop a Funding Request 51
    Funding Source 51
    Equipment and Resources 51
    Loans, Grants and Equity 51
    Adequate Funding 52

STEP 9 – Identify and List Startup Costs 58
    Equipment and Materials 58
    Calculate and Itemize all Costs 58

STEP 10 – Prepare Financial Projections 63
    Financial Statements 63
    Pricing Strategy 64

ENTREPRENEUR'S ROAD MAP

Break-Even Analysis 69
Monitoring Performance 70
Scaling Up 71
Concluding Statement 77

ENTREPRENEUR'S ROAD MAP

ENTREPRENEUR'S ROAD MAP

Introduction and Overview

Introduction and Overview

The idea for this book, "**ENTREPRENEUR'S ROAD MAP** 10 KEY STEPS FOR PREPARING YOUR BUSINESS PLAN," came from recognizing the need most entrepreneurs have for a step-by-step guide. My experience in leading the business planning process gave me a real appreciation for how important it is to a company's success to follow what is identified in a clearly developed and implemented business plan. This book contains how to prepare your business plan.

What is a business plan?

As an entrepreneur, a business owner, a company president or Chief Executive Officer (CEO) you have a passion or purpose for the business you manage or want to start. This passion or purpose is often translated into a mission, a vision and ultimate outlook for your business.

A business plan is an important document to be used for managing your business to help achieve the mission or vision for the organization. The business plan represents the road map for conducting business. You should be able to use it to identify the objectives that are crucial to the overall success of your business.

In developing your business plan, you are expected to identify how you will achieve your mission by serving your customers with your products or services.

Your primary business focus should be very clear to readers of the plan. The readers and users of the document are likely to include

Introduction and Overview

employees, investors and prospective funders. You will often be required to present a business plan if you are seeking funding from lending institutions, investors or business partners.

As the person creating the business plan or being responsible for its development, it is imperative that you understand the various aspects of the business. Use this book as a comprehensive guide as you chart your path to success.

How do I start?

Your take off point will depend on your status prior to beginning your business plan. There are several ways that you may decide to start a new business or continue an existing one. Let's consider four possibilities.

Case 1: You may have jumped right in, already started your business and are currently figuring out the process as you move forward.

Case 2: You may have researched different options for starting a business over several months and now you feel the moment is right for you to get involved in the planning process.

Case 3: You may have retired or left a corporate job and decided to focus on a business in which you are proficient and have always had an interest. You have now moved that passion directly into establishing your own business.

Case 4: You have a few weeks to develop a business plan, to meet an impending commitment, with a focus on supporting your overall mission and vision.

Introduction and Overview

With any of these cases, I recommend using a standard 10-step format for framing the business plan.

First, type up the following headings: (1) Executive Summary, (2) Company Description, (3) Market Strategy and Analysis, (4) Products and Services, (5) Marketing and Sales Plan, (6) Operations Plan (7) Management and Organizational Plan, (8) Funding Request, (9) Startup Expenses and (10) Financial Projections.

After you have written or typed these headings you can move to the next phase of completing the content by following the general guidance given in chapters 1 through 10 of this book.

Why do I need to write a business plan?
When you write down a goal or a plan it is more likely that if you review that goal or plan on a regular basis, you will get it done. When you create your business plan you are conveying that you want to take an organized approach to developing your business. The plan is also a document to share with your investors. You will want to motivate, inspire and provide stakeholders with reasons for supporting or investing in your business. You want to share the information contained with your business partners. Using a business plan is a way of targeting and focusing on the business' mission.

How should a business plan be used?
A business plan should be written with the intent of being used on a regular basis to guide your actions. You should refer to it often and rely on it as a source for tracking those initiatives and planned actions you wanted to complete. I feel very strongly about maximizing the use of a business plan having led business planning efforts in some major profitable and successful companies.

Introduction and Overview

These companies were successful because they:
- clearly defined their strategic objectives that aligned with their missions.
- used the business planning process to track and monitor progress and performance.
- used the focus on achieving goals in the business plans as a way of ensuring accountability among personnel.
- achieved their financial and internal objectives and goals consistently by having an organized process.

What are the steps after writing the business plan?

After the business plan has been written and approved, it should be put into action and should be revised and updated regularly.

The leaders of the organization often want to reassess their business plans midyear to see how the company is performing. I encourage you to review your business plan monthly and determine if you are achieving your projected targets, goals and objectives. You will start to get a sense if the targets are too conservative or too aggressive. You may then take the necessary steps to adjust those targets.

After the first year's performance, reevaluate your business plan and determine what additional items you would like to change or put in place for the next year. The business plan is normally prepared for periods of three to five years and revised every year.

Remember, as you write your business plan you will be developing a plan primarily for building working connections between the owner, employees and customers as depicted in Figure 1 below.

Introduction and Overview

Figure 1 – Building Connections

In the next chapters, we will cover the basic sections of the business plan in more detail. Let's get started.

Chapter 1 – Executive Summary

STEP 1 – Prepare an Executive Summary

Synopsis of Management Expectations

The first section of the business plan is the executive summary which provides a synopsis of management's business perspective, including the focus for achieving the mission and vision. The business focus should be directed toward delighting the customers and providing excellence in products and services to the target market.

The executive summary should be convincing and should deliver a positive, precise, uplifting and encouraging message. You want to appeal to your readers and sell them on the value of your business. There should be emphasis on how customers and clients will benefit from the products/services offered. Upon reading the business plan, potential lenders or investors should have a good sense that they will be able to recover any funds loaned and receive a return on their investments. In simple terms, your business plan should be appealing.

Purpose, Goals, Mission and Vision

In the executive summary, you should specify your overall purpose and why the business will be successful. Start by describing your goals. What are your objectives? What is your overall mission and vision for the business? If you have not yet done so, take the time to formulate a clear mission and vision statement. Here's how:

i) Write the mission statement and explain what it means in simple terms.

Chapter 1 – Executive Summary

ii) Write the vision for the business and explain how you plan to achieve it. Your vision is aspirational and is a statement on how you want your business to be viewed long-term.

iii) Identify how you want to meet the needs of the customers and other stakeholders.

iv) Discuss the products and services you will provide to customers and identify what your target market is going to be. For example, will the market be for people between the ages of 18 and 35? It is best if you identify your target market and customers.

This executive summary section should also give a sense of your leadership team and what specific expertise and experience the team members must have to provide a competitive advantage for your company.

If you have employees, discuss the type of personnel that you will be hiring in the business and describe the ways they will be committed to customers.

Let's examine a sample of a few pages from the business plan for a company we call The Great Shoe Company. Figure 2 shows you an example of the cover page for the plan, while Figures 3 and 4 give you an example of the table of contents and executive summary, respectively. Remember to include basic information, such as your company address and contact details on the cover page. Using the table of contents to list the key elements contained in your business plan up front makes it easy for potential investors to quickly find all the information they need to make their decision to come onboard.

Chapter 1 – Executive Summary

Figure 2 – Business Plan Cover Page Example

```
The Great Shoe Company
Business Plan
31 Stylish Lane
Anytown, NY USA
```

You will want to summarize, in this section, financial projections such as overall revenue and profitability. Here's an example: "We expect to make a profit in the third year of the business because during the first year we'll be ramping up and acquiring more customers." The claims you make here will be expanded upon in the body of the business plan.

The financial projection numbers identified in the executive summary should reflect a high-level synopsis of what you anticipate your overall results will be.

Chapter 1 – Executive Summary

Figure 3 – Business Plan Table of Contents Example

---

1. Executive Summary
2. Company Description
3. Market Strategy
4. Products and Services
5. Marketing and Sales Plan
6. Operations Plan
7. Management Plan
8. Funding Request
9. Startup Plan
10. Financial Projections

Page 1 of 14

Describe any special arrangements you have in place to ensure that the employees or contractors add to the focus of customer satisfaction for your business.

Chapter 1 – Executive Summary

Figure 4 – Sample Executive Summary

> 1. Executive Summary
>
> 1.1 Purpose: The Great Shoe Company is an upscale high quality dress footwear supplier for customers throughout the continental United States
>
> 1.2 Mission: Our mission is to provide our customers exotic high quality, comfortable and durable footwear.
>
> 1.3 We provide a wide assortment of footwear, and we are focused on the sector of the market that are often looking for comfortable and affordable priced shoes. 90% of our market is between the age of 25 and 45. Our current 5-year plan is to expand our market from 5% to 10% of on-line shoppers.

Discuss how the employees will have to be trained adequately in terms of how they're going to fulfill the customers' needs. Again, it is important to be succinct but clear. Although the executive summary appears first in your business plan it's often finalized last because the content is based on the conclusions from the other sections of the document.

Chapter 1 – Executive Summary

Key Points From This Chapter

- Provide a synopsis of the management perspective.
- How will the mission and vision be achieved by delighting the customer?
- How will you meet your goals and objectives?
- How will you meet your target market needs?
- What are the expected financial results upon delivering customer value?

Chapter 1 – Executive Summary

Learnings to Take Away 1

List a few things you've learned from this chapter.

List items that represent the primary purpose of your business.

Chapter 1 – Executive Summary

What is the mission of your business?

List those you believe will be your typical customers.

Chapter 2 - Company Description

STEP 2 – Share Your Company Description

Type of Business and Structure
The company description is where you give details about your business structure. In this section, include the name of your business and the location. If you are operating from different addresses and it is critical to the customers, they will want to know the locations in which you operate. You should indicate the type of business you own. State whether you are a "doing business as" (DBA), a sole proprietor, a partnership, a corporation, or a limited liability company (LLC). This description will be based on how you registered the business in your state.

Expertise and Strength
People will want to know if you have a sound business and if they can reach you. Remember to identify the specific personnel skills and management expertise you will be using to remain competitive in meeting customers' needs. State if your organization does business face-to-face, online or both. You may include something like "We offer our products and services online only." It is also advisable to list your website address.

Organization History
You may also want to discuss the history of the business. Most people like the idea of telling the story behind how the company was formed, evolved, or grew to where it is currently. Potential funders find such details interesting.

Chapter 2 - Company Description

If the business is a startup, you should mention that. People in the community will want to help the business grow if they are excited about it. If the company does well, the community will also benefit. Ensure that in discussing the history, you provide an understanding of why the company took on its mission and vision.

You'll notice that the mission and vision will be referred to several times throughout this guidebook. This should give an indication that you definitely want to detail your mission and vision and state how you will achieve them.

On average, about half a page should be adequate for the company description. This may well be the shortest section in your business plan. Figure 5 shows a simple example of the content that should be included in this section. A brief overview of the company, the goals, the values and the target market should be included.

Chapter 2 - Company Description

Figure 5 – Sample Company Description

> This is a simple example for illustration purposes only. Your company description will be relevant to your business and will be a section in your business plan. Let us use the XYZ Company as an example.
>
> **2.0 Company Description**
>
> The **XYZ Company** is a for profit Limited Liability Company (LLC) registered in New York State. Our main facilities are located at 31 Stylish Lane, Anytown New York. We operated initially as a doing business as (DBA) and has now registered as an LLC. The company started in 20XX and is progressively building to develop a lucrative market in footwear sales by offering more comfortable and high-quality durable products.
>
> Our customers service staff are well trained individuals that are focused day-to-day on offering exceptional service and support. Our founder and CEO is fully committed to our company delivering high quality through our customer satisfaction programs (CSP).
>
> The **XYZ Company** sells shoes on a wholesale and retail basis to customers across the United States. We distribute our products online and through independent contract sales staff. In the next two years we intend to operate distribution facilities in Chicago, Illinois and San Diego California.

Chapter 2 - Company Description

Key Points From This Chapter

- Identify your company by name.
- List the state in which the business is registered.
- Discuss the location of any facilities you have.
- Include the history of how your business started.

Chapter 2 - Company Description

Learnings to Take Away 2

How do you plan to set up your business as a legal entity?

List any plans you have for your company to grow and expand.

Chapter 2 - Company Description

List any thoughts about how you want your company to operate from its current location.

Make notes on the history of your business.

Chapter 3 - Market Strategy and Analysis

STEP 3 – Outline Market Strategy and Analysis

Developing a marketing strategy can take quite a bit of research, especially if yours is a new business. Based on what you discovered from your research you can then formulate your marketing strategy. You want to understand what the demands are for your products and services. Discuss the expected desire your customers should have for your products or services and state why. This desire should ultimately drive the demand for your products and services somewhere in the industry. Ensure that you also address questions related to the market size and how much of that market you intend to capture. Your research may include census data that would help you to define the potential market size.

Demographics

You will want to examine available economic indicators including income ranges of people within the general demographic area that will be buying your products and or services. Do you know the people that will mostly buy your products based on your pricing? Discuss the expected affordability of those products or services. How do you obtain this research data? Your public library is one of the best sources of information. Your librarians can provide very good guidance on where to look. You can then broaden your search on the Internet.

Chapter 3 - Market Strategy and Analysis

Target Market
You need to emphasize why you are targeting that sector of the market. You should have discussion points to address areas such as why you think you could participate in that market sector at the specified price point. Again, identify what value you are offering or what problem you're solving.

As a business, are you entering a market that is saturated? If it is, what are your plans to remain competitive and be successful? This issue is worth doing some brainstorming with others on your team or within your network.

Pricing
As part of your marketing strategy of course you will discuss the pricing. Determine what potential customers would be willing to pay for an alternative product. What if an alternative product provides the same value that your product is providing but it's for a lower price? How will you compete against that alternative product? What added value do you have over the competition? You must understand and address what the competitors are doing. It is well worth visiting your competitors to see how they conduct business and determine if there is something you could learn.

Research and Surveys
Some direct research is also important. You could do that through conducting surveys. Use a list of emails for your potential customers to deliver the questionnaire. Sending out specific surveys to that sector of the market will help you get a sense of how many people are ready to buy your products and services and how many are looking for the features that you offer. Consider who may be your ideal customer. It is a good idea when you do a survey with potential

Chapter 3 - Market Strategy and Analysis

clients to ask them what they like. Keep the surveys brief to ensure that your response rate is up, even for very busy individuals.

You can also conduct focus groups by inviting potential and existing customers to provide feedback related to your products and services. They can be interviewed in a room or auditorium setting. You could also set up a virtual discussion forum during which you may ask specific questions about the product that you plan to offer. Survey responses and feedback on your products or services and what customers like about them are very important for you to know.

Customer interviews are extremely valuable. Virtual or face-to-face interviews give you an opportunity to hear the responses and observe the body language.

Some businesses are hesitant to send out surveys asking for customers' feedback about a particular product or service. One of the reasons given is that the customers may provide information that the business owner does not want to hear.

Business owners should welcome opportunities for getting feedback on how the business could improve. Surveys provide information that could help the business take corrective steps early and not wait until there is a major problem.

Chapter 3 - Market Strategy and Analysis

Think about all the ways you can and will be interacting with the consumers and obtaining valuable information. These are considered as customer touch points. Figure 6 below shows some of those touchpoints. Use these as starting points to learn more about your consumers' needs and wants.

Figure 6 – Customer Touchpoints

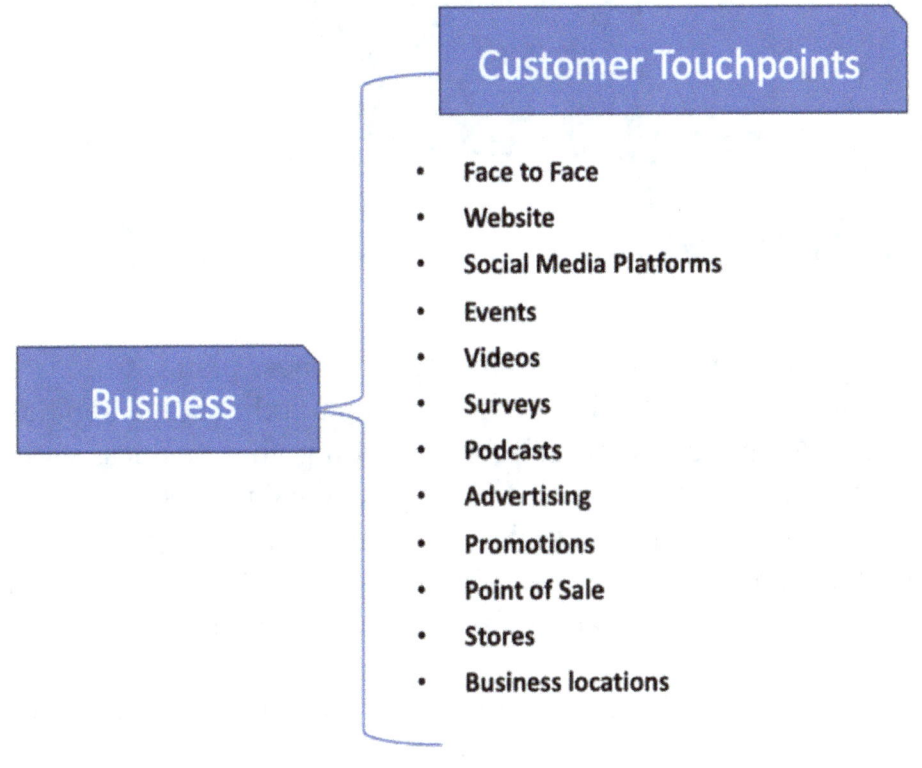

Chapter 3 - Market Strategy and Analysis

Competitive Analysis Including SWOT

Figure 7 – Components of SWOT Analysis

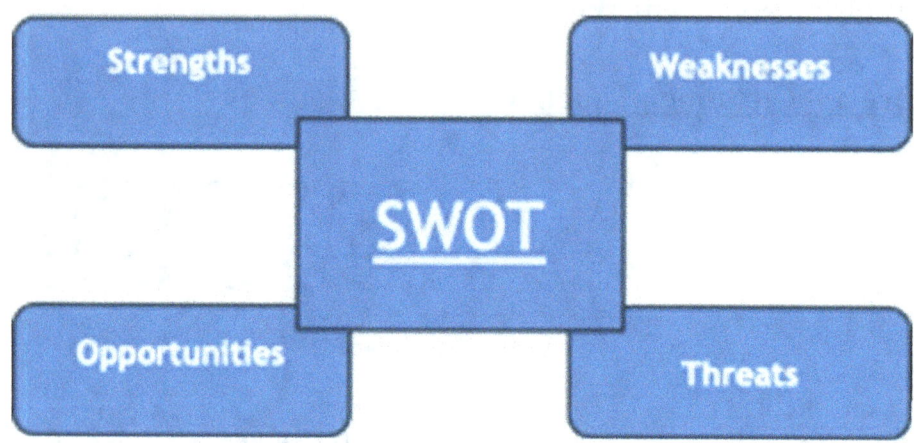

Another important part of developing a business plan is to determine how your business measures up to other players in the industry. A standard approach for comparing your business with the competitors is to perform a Strengths, Weaknesses, Opportunities and Threats (SWOT) analysis. Assessing these four important aspects of your business, as shown in Figure 7, is key to devising a successful strategy for the future. Here's how:

First, document your core strengths as a business. How do these compare with your competitors? You will need to look at about two to four of your competitors and consider your strengths, while you review theirs. You may have a particular expertise that very few people in this area have. So, it is feasible that you are relying heavily on your skills to offer the products and services of your business. This expertise could be considered one of your strengths. You may

Chapter 3 - Market Strategy and Analysis

have a patent for a product. Owning the patented process, especially if you're the only one that owns the patent, provides an advantage over the competitors. This should be discussed as part of your business plan.

Other strengths include the analytical and leadership ability of employees that you'll be hiring or already have in place. Any significant advantage that you believe you have should be identified among your strengths.

Similarly, you should look at any weaknesses in your business. Maybe you are new in the market. Do you have to build up a certain amount of expertise for your products and services to reach customers? If you are just starting out, chances are you may have to compete against well-established enterprises. When you look at the weaknesses, the objective is not to feel bad about them, but to understand what they are and put processes in place for addressing them.

Next, review potential opportunities that are becoming available for your business and identify those which allow you to gain advantage. Here are some steps you could take to ensure that you are in alignment with new possibilities:

- Consider registering with organizations that will lead you to customers who will need your products and services. This includes the local chamber of commerce and organizations that accept bidding from businesses.
- Participate in and attend conferences where there are opportunities to promote your products and services.

Chapter 3 - Market Strategy and Analysis

- Read the journals or local newspapers that advertise new businesses. Set up a process as part of your operations that you will use to contact those new business owners.

Let's move on to threats, examples of which may include a deteriorating economic condition. The pandemic was a real threat to many businesses. Those that could pivot and go from a brick-and-mortar type focus to selling online, had less difficulty getting their products and services to customers. Others were not as lucky.

What type of products and services are you offering? Are you offering essential services or are you offering products and services that only few people would really need during hard economic conditions? If you have a seasonal business, you may identify a unique set of issues for your business plan. Your business must be functioning best at the peak season. You cannot afford to have lengthy downtimes then. Resolution of downtime during these periods then would be of high priority to you.

It is important to evaluate how your business will perform whether the economy is good or bad and establish contingency plans. One situation may be beneficial for one business and a disadvantage for another. For example, if there is a severe weather condition that causes a business to lose power, more people would be interested in installing generators at their businesses to keep things going.

However, as the owner of an electric generator business, you will find your product to be in greater demand at that point when people need it. But there may also be a quiet market that you could pursue which would include new builders. Can you get the homeowner or home buyer to even think about getting a generator ahead of time, rather than after they have built their homes and had some

Chapter 3 - Market Strategy and Analysis

experiences with a power outage? What about forward-planning business owners? Are they a good market for you to pursue?

These are just a few of the situations and conditions to keep in mind as you make your assessment and develop your strategy.

If I am thinking of funding your enterprise and I look at your SWOT analysis, I will examine the weaknesses and threats and balance them against the strengths and opportunities. As a business owner you should be prepared for various situations that may arise. It will serve you well to identify potential challenges and the actions you will need to take to resolve those challenges.

Market Share

In this section of the business plan, you will need to address key factors such as what market share you aim to capture. If there are other competitors in the field, what are the chances of you getting 2% or 1% of the market in your industry?

Is a 1% market share sufficient to meet your financial objectives? Ensure that you analyze the numbers realistically and ask yourself the following: Do I want to be in this space? Should I really specialize in this area? Is this my window of opportunity to enter the market? What is the best time to enter the market from a cash flow standpoint? Are there any specific barriers to me entering the market? Are there options for resolving these issues as part of my business plan?

The answers to these questions should be addressed in your marketing analysis along with the specific actions you plan to take. You must look at the needs of your customers based on the sector of the market in which your business operates. This is significant

Chapter 3 - Market Strategy and Analysis

regardless of whether you are in food service, engineering, construction, education, government, health care, technology or other types of businesses where you plan to accomplish your objectives and mission.

Added Value and Competitive Advantage

Again, you're going to review the details of your products and services and describe the benefits that you bring to the table. What is the value proposition that you want to deliver to the customers? Why will the customers give rave reviews about your products and services? Identify how you can deliver that value for a price.

Will your customers be able to talk about how you have changed their life or lifestyle? If you're already in business and have received testimonials from customers, consider including a few of their words to state how you intend to satisfy additional customers' needs as part of your business plan.

Key Points From This Chapter

- What is the market size of the business you are pursuing?
- What does your research reveal about the real need for your business?
- Is the trend for your business in the industry increasing or decreasing?
- Who are your competitors and how well are they doing?
- What customer demographics are you pursuing?
- Do you plan to do surveys or focus groups?
- What are the strengths, weaknesses, opportunities and threats your company may have?
- What competitive advantages do you have?

Chapter 3 - Market Strategy and Analysis

Learnings to Take Away 3

Why do you think a market strategy is important to your business?

How do you think you could outperform your competitors?

Chapter 3 - Market Strategy and Analysis

What ideas came to you about analyzing your market?

What resources will you be using to analyze your business and the industry?

Chapter 4 - Products and Services

STEP 4 – Describe Your Products and Services

Use this section to give the particulars of your products and services. If you are selling several items, you will want to discuss each of the major categories in detail in terms of the offerings you are providing and the value to the customers. Describe why you selected each category of product or service and how each one compares with what your competitors offer.

Value and Benefits

Explain how the products or services will satisfy the overall sector of the market. Provide an overview of how your products and services are priced. If you have multiple items, create a table showing them and a comparison of the main features as shown in Figure 8 below. Consistent with the information depicted in the figure, give a clear visual display of your pricing structure.

Describe the benefits of your products and services to the customers. If the products and services meet the customers' needs, your next task would be to ensure that there is exceptional customer service. Your ability to provide quality products and services should be emphasized in this section of the business plan. The coupling of excellent products and services with timely delivery of the same is a key element of having a sustainable business.

Chapter 4 - Products and Services

Figure 8 – Products/Services Pricing and Benefit Chart

Products/ Services	Price	Features	Advantages/ Benefits
Product A			
Product B			
Service A			
Service B			

Key Points From This Chapter

- What are your products/services?
- What value do you bring to customers?
- What are the main benefits you offer?
- How does your pricing compare with other similar businesses?

Chapter 4 - Products and Services

Learnings to Take Away 4

What steps will you take to make your products and services more desirable to the customers?

List some specific benefits of your products and services.

Chapter 4 - Products and Services

What other companies sell similar products or offer the services that you do?

List items in your pricing plan that needs to be addressed.

Chapter 5- Marketing and Sales Plan

STEP 5 – Discuss Marketing and Sales Plan

What are your plans for selling your products and marketing your business? How would you identify those plans to attract and retain customers? How are you going to advertise? Will you be advertising in print, on social media, through a website or other platform? You could put some effort into organic marketing, where you develop a community through blogging, podcasting or other means of sharing your experience, as it seems to really help the pace at which you can grow. These are all key areas to consider as you develop a solid strategy.

Website and Videos
How effectively will you use a website to advertise and encourage customers to review your products and services? Remember, your website sits dormant until someone visits and acts. Identify those items that you will put in place to attract customers to your website and trigger action. Is the site up to date? Is it user-friendly? When customers come to the website do they enjoy the experience? Consider incorporating videos on the site to educate customers about your products and services. There is a real opportunity here to build connections.

Promotions
One important decision you need to make as a business owner is how much paid promotions you can afford compared to free media. Take some time to address the questions above. Include the answers to these in developing your marketing plan.

Chapter 5- Marketing and Sales Plan

Collaboration

Give some consideration to how much you can collaborate with other businesses. Think about this in terms of how your products and services will complement the other businesses. You will be able to share the cost of putting on events and building relationships aimed at increasing and supporting each business entity.

Sales Projections

Develop a sales plan by identifying the quantity of products and services you intend to sell each month. Ascertain the cost of delivering each product and service and then determine your monthly and yearly income projections.

Ensure that you have a monthly projection of your expected sales. As an example, the projected sales for shoes and boots and service contracts are shown for the coming year in Figure 9 for one store, the Great Shoe Company, in one location. This sales projection will help you forecast revenue. Think through and identify ways of increasing your sales and attracting customers. You may consider special offerings and incentives, including establishing a customer loyalty program.

Chapter 5- Marketing and Sales Plan

Figure 9 – Expected Sales Projections

Sales Projection of footwear and service contracts (20XX)												
	Jan	Feb	Mar	Apr	May	Jun	Jul	Aug	Sep	Oct	Nov	Dec
Shoes	25	35	35	40	40	55	32	32	60	60	100	120
Boots	15	15	10	10	10	12	12	15	15	25	30	40
Service Contracts	5	5	7	7	7	10	10	10	10	10	10	15

Key Points From This Chapter

- What is your plan for reaching customers?
- How do you plan to do promotions such as advertising and videos?
- What is your sales plan?
- How much sales will you generate weekly, monthly and yearly?
- What kind of incentive program do you have for ensuring customers purchase?
- Have you identified a list of social media platforms you will be using?

Chapter 5- Marketing and Sales Plan

Learnings to Take Away 5

What ideas will you use from this book to expand your market?

Which of your products or services could you sell best?

Chapter 5- Marketing and Sales Plan

Sketch out your idea for a monthly sales plan.

List any other support you need to ensure you meet your goals.

Chapter 6 - Operations Plan

STEP 6 – Provide an Overview of Operations Plan

What is the importance of having an operations plan?

The operations plan will cover your process for getting the product or service ready to be delivered to the customers. The discussion in this section will include those actions you intend to take to ensure that the products and services are of the highest quality.

> Note: *If your business does not manufacture products, certain sections of the operations plan may not apply to you. If you are a service business and you do not deliver a tangible product, it is still worth understanding the process.*

If you manufacture products as part of your business, ensure that you address the level of quality that will be delivered. Your process from manufacturing, assembling, packaging and shipping to customers should include certain key criteria and metrics. For example, how will you make sure that your services remain relevant and meet the current customers' needs? If your location will be important in terms of delivery of the products and services, discuss this here.

Shipping

A crucial area to review and address in your business plan is how you will handle shipping. Are you going to use United Parcel Services (UPS), Federal Express (FedEx), the United States Postal Services (USPS), Amazon or other shipping companies to ensure prompt and safe delivery of your goods? This logistical detail needs to be resolved early on.

Chapter 6 - Operations Plan

Damaged Goods

It is also essential to discuss how any damage to your customers' products will be addressed. Is there any kind of money-back guarantee that will be set up? It is good to decide on a customer satisfaction policy and state what it is in your business plan.

Inventory

If you look at the inventory for the goods it is important to have proper shelf-life management so that there are no losses due to spoiled products. Another aspect of managing inventory is to ensure there is sufficient product availability to avoid backlogs. If you're a sole entrepreneur, remember you wear several hats. Determine if you will need additional staff to handle product issues. Will you get someone to come in to check that your products are available or are you going to order what is called "just in time"? If you get your products made by an outside manufacturer, you may order enough so that you will receive the products in time to deliver to your customers. It is prudent, however, to consider a backup plan to identify and address delays.

Suppliers/Payments

Will you be sending products directly to the customers or are you going to operate on a drop ship basis? How will you work with your suppliers? Ensure that as a business you have a way to pay suppliers on time. It is important to keep them satisfied. Remember that they must pay their bills, too. There is a strong chance that you will have a very good working relationship with suppliers that get paid as promised. Consider some of the challenges you will have if your suppliers go out of business. Do you currently have a list of alternate suppliers?

Chapter 6 - Operations Plan

Credit Policy

Within your business plan you need to address your credit policy with respect to your customers. Does the customer receive the product and then pay you later or do you collect cash up front? Protect the certainty of your revenue by collecting your payment up front whenever you can.

Addressing how you deal with payments to suppliers and from customers will ensure that you have some consistency in operating your business.

Key Points From This Chapter

- Identify processes and procedures from the time you receive an order to delivery.
- Have a strategy for maintaining high quality in your products and services.
- Determine how you plan to get your products/services to customers.
- If you must carry inventory, identify the level to be carried that is not costly.
- Determine your established payment and collection process.
- If you have suppliers, include a list of alternate suppliers.
- Develop a customer satisfaction process.

Chapter 6 - Operations Plan

Learnings to Take Away 6

List ideas you have for processing or offering your products/services effectively.

List items that could prevent your processes from working smoothly.

Chapter 6 - Operations Plan

List solutions for addressing the items that could hamper progress.

What other items will be important to your operations?

Chapter 7 – Management and Organization Plan

STEP 7 – Present a Management Plan

Leadership Team

As the owner or CEO of a business, one of your primary objectives should be to have an engaging leadership team. As an individual entrepreneur who is just starting out you may not have such a team currently in place. However, it is never too early to think about how you want to grow the business in three to five years and the personnel it will take to help you get there. A business owner needs to have a management team with the proper leadership, planning and communication skills. For now, it's acceptable to discuss this team in terms of where you want it to be in the long term.

Structure

The structure of your business may look like that shown in Figure 10 and you can then grow from there. If you have a small business, you may be the founder, owner, and president. In this case, you may want to start out with an external bookkeeper to maintain and keep track of your financial records and then submit it to an accountant at the end of the year.

Chapter 7 – Management and Organization Plan

Figure 10 – Management Organization Chart

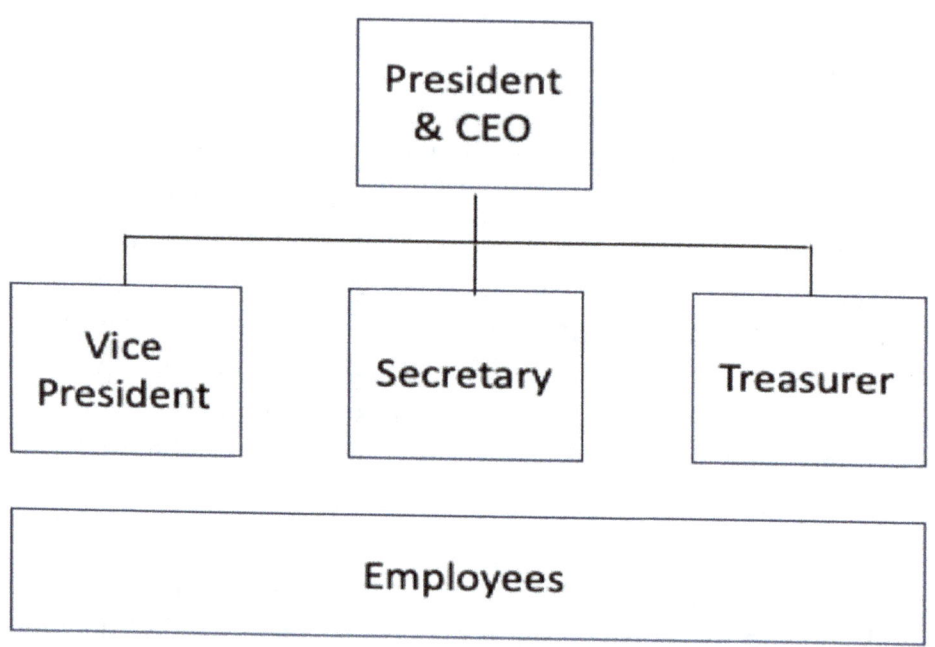

As your business grows, it will be beneficial to have an administrative assistant to help manage the key aspects of your company including organizing and supporting meeting the customers' needs. You may also have a co-owner or vice president as a second person that will help you manage your business.

Looking at the processes within your business and determining how you could use technology to improve efficiency, is also an invaluable exercise.

As entrepreneurs, we are often optimistic about how much we could independently accomplish. This optimism could lead to a business

Chapter 7 – Management and Organization Plan

owner taking on more responsibilities and not establishing a management team and organization structure. Consider establishing the organization structure for major areas of responsibilities where you need help in operating your enterprise effectively.

Including an organization chart that shows areas of responsibilities and the reporting structure is a good way to go. Readers of your business plan should get an indication of how your business will be managed. As a business, it is important to have adequate staffing to support your customer base. It is equally as important that as your business develops more of the desired structure there is a true balance with the financial means to grow.

If you have an advisory group or board of directors, this will also help to ensure there are fresh ideas and proper oversight in place for your business.

Compensation

As a business owner, it is important that you consider how you will compensate personnel on your leadership team. It is often advantageous to compensate personnel on the level of performance of the business. If the business does well the personnel can be compensated based on their level of contribution to its success. Using this process tends to incentivize employees to do well.

Businesses are often most vulnerable during the initial startup phase, so the business owner may need to provide less generous compensation then.

You should balance compensation based on the level of profitability that your business can sustain.

Chapter 7 – Management and Organization Plan

Key Points From This Chapter

- List personnel on the leadership team. Include your planned assignments.
- Identify responsibilities for vital areas.
- Map out the organization structure.
- Map out a three- to five-year growth plan.
- Identify the compensation process.

Chapter 7 – Management and Organization Plan

Learnings to Take Away 7

List individuals who would be a good fit for your management team.

List individuals that would be good as your advisors.

Chapter 7 – Management and Organization Plan

What are key positions that you need to fill in your business?

List other thoughts you have about the management and organization plan.

Chapter 8 – Funding Request

STEP 8 – Develop a Funding Request

Funding Source

If you will be seeking funding for your business from external sources, you should address this in your business plan. After working through all the earlier written sections in the document, it is worth using a disciplined approach to identify how much funding you will need and how you will be using those funds. Investors and loan institutions want assurance that the money you borrow will be used effectively and that they will receive a reasonable return on their investments.

Equipment and Resources

List the cost of equipment, materials, paying salaries, marketing, and other relevant items as you detail the funding needs. This will be of major interest to those individuals or organizations providing the financing.

Loans, Grants and Equity

Funding may be in the form of loans or grants. Loans require that you pay back the lender. Grants do not require repayment, but often have stipulations as to how the money is to be used. You will also want to include a description of any plans you have in the future for paying off debt or selling your business.

Determine if you intend to use your own money, try to secure loans or will seek investors. Do you want a partner to invest in your business? You will also need to determine how that person will get a return on their investment.

Chapter 8 – Funding Request

Will your business be funded with debt or equity? Ensure you understand the terms and conditions of any loans you obtain.

If you do get a loan, the lower the interest rate the better it will be for you to pay it back. If you have a fixed rate, you will have more control over your payments. Be sure that if you acquire a loan, it is built into your financial projections, and you can manage monthly payments or whatever is required. Find out how much actual interest you are paying on the loan. A shortened period, low fixed interest rate loan will lead you to pay less interest in total.

It is imperative that you thoroughly understand the terms of any loan. Be careful when it comes to variable rates. Ensure you understand if such a rate has a cap so that you can manage the resulting payments.

Adequate Funding
Starting a business can become challenging if you encounter problems with underfunding. Signs of not being fully funded include having trouble purchasing the necessary equipment, finding the best business location and hiring personnel.

Being underfunded can affect paying for day-to-day operation expenses, and your ability to expand and meet those key objectives that will make your business more competitive and profitable. You will need sufficient funding to properly launch and stay on track as a viable business.

Chapter 8 – Funding Request

As a business owner, if you fully discuss those items identified in this section, you should be ready to prepare a funding request. Since funding requests can take many forms, I recommend putting your appeal in the form of a letter. The main purpose of this example letter is to address key requirements that need to be included for a company we call "Education XYZ" as shown in Figure 11.

Chapter 8 – Funding Request

Figure 11 – Funding Request Example

> **Purpose:** The purpose of this letter is to seek funding to cover our startup and six-month operational expense for a new business "Education XYZ".
>
> **Company Objective:** Education XYZ is a for-profit company in western New York. We provide computer-based training for a suite of financial business software to be used by students including adult learners. Our objective is to make individuals more proficient in using computer software in their personal and professional lives.
>
> **Details of Requested Funds:** We are seeking a grant or low interest funding of $150,000 to cover the following items of our business:
>
> **Startup Cost**
>
> | | |
> |---|---|
> | Initial Personnel Training | - $ 20,000 |
> | Classroom Furniture | - $ 56,000 |
> | Building Renovation | - $ 74,000 |
> | **Total** | **$150,000** |
>
> This funding is necessary for our initial startup and for addressing operations expenses during the first few months of being in business. Our 3-year financial statements projections are attached for your review in our business plan.
>
> We plan to repay the loan over 7 years. Please let us know if there is any additional information that you may require.
>
> Thanks for taking the time to review our request.

Chapter 8 – Funding Request

Key Points From This Chapter

- Identify the areas of your business for which you need internal or external funding.
- Determine who are potential funders.
- Determine the requirements around funding sources (loans, grants or equity).
- What percent of funding is expected from each source?
- Develop a plan for using the funds obtained.

Chapter 8 – Funding Request

Learnings to Take Away 8

What are some ideas you have for obtaining funding?

Which organizations could be possible funding sources for your business?

Chapter 8 – Funding Request

List the important dates by which you will need funding.

List actions you need to take to seek business funding.

Chapter 9 – Startup Costs

STEP 9 – Identify and List Startup Costs

Equipment and Materials

As an entrepreneur or owner looking at any new business, you will need to consider the startup costs. These represent the funds that are required prior to opening the business. Map out all items you will need when you start up your business. You want to ensure that you are in a good position to service your customers effectively. If you do not clearly identify and address required startup funding for your business, it is likely to impact the availability of cash and your ability to acquire equipment or materials that are crucial for business operations.

Some of the essential startup costs are for office space, initial rental, security deposit, equipment, supplies, communications, utilities, licenses, permits, insurance, lawyer and accountant fees, inventory costs, employees' certifications, initial salary, advertising, marketing, and the cost of paying for a website.

Calculate and Itemize all Costs.

It is very important that you calculate and understand the total startup costs before you begin your business. It is best if these costs are clearly itemized in your business plan.

Chapter 9 – Startup Costs

Figure 12 – Startup Costs Example for ABC Company

STARTUP COST: ABC Company	
Description	Budgeted Cost
Personnel:	
Training	$ 100
Certification	$ 500
Lawyers Fee	$ 3,000
Accountant Fee	$ 1,500
Equipment and Supplies:	
Office Furniture	$ 25,000
Licenses	$ 300
Computer and Internet	$ 4,500
Utilities	$ 750
Website	$ 1,500
Marketing & Promotions	$ 1,000
Facilities:	
Office Building Renovation	$ 30,000
Lease and Security Deposit	$ 7,000
Permits	$ 250
Total Startup Costs	**$ 75,400**

Chapter 9 – Startup Costs

Key Points From This Chapter

- Determine all your startup costs.
- Identify major items of equipment, furniture, facilities and personnel you need prior to starting up.
- Itemize cost for the equipment, furniture and facilities as well as personnel.

Chapter 9 – Startup Costs

Learnings to Take Away 9

List some of the items you will need to start your business.

List facilities you could visit to review equipment or furniture.

Chapter 9 – Startup Costs

List any personnel training to be done prior to starting up.

Any other items required before your business can start?

Chapter 10 – Financial Projections

STEP 10 – Prepare Financial Projections

It's time to prepare financial inputs for your business plan. You will need to review your expected monthly income, expenses and cash flow, and estimate the yearly dollar amounts for at least three years. Similarly, you will need to review the assets and the liabilities and state how you plan to fund your business.

Financial Statements

Working with an expert, you will be able to arrive at projected financial statements which include income statements, balance sheets and cash flow statements. The overall statements represent your projection into the future and are referred to as "financial projections."

The financial projections are crucial in determining how you plan to succeed. Some of these projections will be estimates or quoted costs. Gathering estimates is a disciplined approach to considering the financials for both long-term and short-term objectives in your business.

When you examine the financial projections, what you are really doing is assessing why you need to start or continue the business and when you will be successful in generating profits.

Begin by describing your assumptions for the financial projections. Review your startup expenses, your payroll costs and sales forecast. Prepare an income statement, cash flow statement and projected balance sheet. These three statements are your financial statements.

Chapter 10 – Financial Projections

Pricing Strategy

Pricing of your products or services has a direct impact on your income statement and overall profitability. The following are some steps in verifying if you are set up to be profitable.

⇒ 1. Decide on the selling price for your products or services.
⇒ 2. Determine what it will cost you to supply the products or the services. This includes the price for the material, labor and overhead.
⇒ 3. Estimate your sales volume for a year.
⇒ 4. Determine your expected revenue.
⇒ 5. Determine the cost of goods and services.
⇒ 6. Calculate the gross profit.
⇒ 7. Determine your operating expenses.
⇒ 8. Determine if gross profit will be sufficient to cover the operating expenses.

Chapter 10 – Financial Projections

Let us take each of the above line items and show you what happens by way of a specific example:

The selling price per unit for a bookcase = $1,500
The cost per unit for building the bookcase = $300

My sales projection for the first three months are:

	Jan	Feb	Mar
Projected Sales Volume	10	15	12

The expected revenue and cost for the projected sales are:

	Jan	Feb	Mar
Projected Revenue	10 x $1,500	15 x $1,500	12 x $1,500
	= $15,000	= $22,500	= $18,000

	Jan	Feb	Mar
Projected Cost of Goods	10 x $300	15 x $300	12 x $300
	= $3,000	= $4,500	= $3,600

Chapter 10 – Financial Projections

The overall revenue for three months is calculated as:
$15,000 + 22,500 + $18,000 = $55,500; and the overall cost of goods for the three months is $3,000 + $4,500 + $3,600 = $11,100.

Revenue	$55,500
Cost of Goods	$11,100
Gross Profit	$44,400

(Note that Revenue minus Cost of Goods is equal to Gross Profit.)

This example was for three months, but the sales projection could be developed for the entire year, and we would then be able to see the gross profit for the entire year. The final step in this process is to look at all additional expenses, termed "operating expenses" the business will incur and ensure that the gross profit can cover the listed expenses. Some typical operating expenses include:

- Salaries
- Office space
- Utilities
- Insurance
- Website development and upkeep
- Accounting fees
- Legal fees
- Marketing
- Advertising
- Supplies
- Travel and entertainment

Chapter 10 – Financial Projections

Based on the business you own; you would need to modify this list and include all additional expenses. If all the other expenses added up to $40,000, the operating profit would be as shown below.

Revenue	$55,500
Cost of Goods	$11,100
Gross Profit	$44,400
Operating Expenses	$40,000
Operating Profit	$ 4,400

This information shown above represents a simple income statement. Note that the income statement is sometimes called a profit and loss (P&L) statement. A copy of the income statement for ABC Motor Repairs is included here in Figure 13 as an example. This is shown for a three-year period.

Chapter 10 – Financial Projections

Figure 13 – 3-year Income Statement Example

ABC Motor Repairs Fiscal Year		2024		2025		2026
Income Statement						
Earned Income						
Revenue - Engines	$	1,000,000	$	1,050,000	$	1,102,500
Revenue - Repair Services	$	312,000	$	327,600	$	343,980
Total Revenue	$	1,312,000	$	1,377,600	$	1,446,480
Cost of Goods - Engines	$	400,000	$	420,000	$	441,000
Cost of Goods - Repair Services	$	124,800	$	131,040	$	137,592
Total Cost of Goods/Service	$	524,800	$	551,040	$	578,592
	$	-	$	-	$	-
Gross Profit Margin	$	787,200	$	826,560	$	867,888
Salary	$	120,000	$	126,000	$	132,300
Training	$	12,000	$	12,600	$	13,230
Business Cards	$	45	$	47	$	50
Rent	$	36,000	$	37,800	$	39,690
Website	$	48,000	$	50,400	$	52,920
Insurance	$	6,000	$	6,300	$	6,615
Supplies	$	8,500	$	8,925	$	9,371
Internet	$	3,600	$	3,780	$	3,969
Utilities	$	18,000	$	18,900	$	19,845
Trade Organization Membership Dues	$	600	$	630	$	662
Accounting Fees	$	1,200	$	1,260	$	1,323
Legal Fees	$	6,000	$	6,300	$	6,615
Public Relations	$	540	$	567	$	595
Marketing	$	2,400	$	2,520	$	2,646
Conferences	$	600	$	630	$	662
LLC Registration & Publication	$	750	$	788	$	827
Travel & Entertainment	$	3,600	$	3,780	$	3,969
Loan Payment	$	32,400	$	34,020	$	35,721
Miscellaneous and Contingency	$	6,000	$	6,300	$	6,615
Operating Expenses	$	306,235	$	321,547	$	337,624
Total EBIT (Operating Profit)	$	480,965	$	505,013	$	530,264

Chapter 10 – Financial Projections

Break-Even Analysis

In your business you will encounter fixed and variable costs. Fixed costs are those that do not change in response to the volume of business done. These include items such as rent, utility and insurance. Variable costs change in proportion to the volume of business being transacted and include such items as material cost and labor costs. Your fixed costs plus variable costs add up to your total costs. In your business, before you make a profit, you must cover those fixed and variable costs. When your total cost is equal to the revenue you are at what is defined as the break-even point. Your business will start to become profitable when revenue levels are above the break-even point.

The cost of goods sold is what it is costing you to either acquire, manufacture, or assemble the products and prepare them for sale. If you offer services, we then refer to the cost of services. If you're purely in a service business, identify what it costs for you to deliver that service. Understanding the financial statements and what they convey about your business is essential. The cost of goods for a product will be made up of what it costs you for materials, labor and overhead that can be directly linked to that product. Some key factors to be considered for your financial statements are:

- The pricing for your products and services.
- The profitability of your business.
- The break-even point in terms of quantity and sales.
- Generating adequate revenue and cash flows.
- Maintaining your balance sheet such that you do not have significant debt that becomes too challenging.

Chapter 10 – Financial Projections

Monitoring Performance

Your management of the financials is so crucial that it is advisable to set up a section in your business plan to monitor key financial measures regularly. Let's look at how to establish a target profit goal. In example A, shown here in Figure 14, we have a goal of achieving 10% profit of $12,000, from the business.

Figure 14 – Establish Desired Profit

Establish Desired Profit

Example A

Revenue =		$120,000
Profit desired =	10% =	$12,000
Maximum Expenses =		$108,000

Example B

Revenue =		$7,000
Profit desired =	8% =	$560
Maximum Expenses =		$6,440

The maximum expense we can incur and still achieve that goal is $108,000. In example B, the revenue level is lower at $7,000. With the desired goal of achieving 8% profit of $560, the maximum expense we can incur is $6,440.

Chapter 10 – Financial Projections

I recommend that you manage the business consistent with what you identified in your business plan. Note that the business plan should be referenced when trying to ensure if your organization is meeting your mission and vision.

Scaling Up

Business owners sometimes ask about what is needed to scale up their businesses. With scaling up you may (1) expand your current base of business or (2) add new products or services to your current business model. As a business owner or manager, you want to make sure you have proper financial accountability prior to scaling up. The best way to ensure such accountability is to start with your financial statements. This is how you will be conveying financially how you plan to manage a profitable business.

Scaling up your business should be attempted after you have a basic understanding of the following:

1. What are your primary products/services and what other products and services could be offered for your current business model or environment?
2. Do you have sufficient funding to expand while maintaining financial stability in your business?
3. Do you currently have a consistent demand for your products and services?
4. Is your business currently profitable? Will the increased demand make you more profitable?
5. Do you have a good understanding of your current process for producing and delivering products and services to your customers?

Chapter 10 – Financial Projections

6. Do you have well-trained employees or contractors that are delivering consistent high-quality services?
7. Will you be able to increase your staff and facilities to meet higher demands for all the anticipated new products and services?

If you could answer yes to the above questions and you have adequate cash flow, then you can consider expanding. It is my opinion that you should not put the business at risk by being consumed by debt.

It is prudent to have a clear way of paying your expenses and meeting your obligations on time. Ensure that scaling up means that you still maintain or expand your competitive advantage. If you encounter challenges in your business, evaluate whether you should (1) continue along the current path, (2) change direction or (3) stop so that you can have your business remain viable. The business should work in your and the stakeholders' best interest.

Your balance sheet reflects the health of your business as you grow. Figure 15 is a sample balance sheet for ASB Company, Inc. The balance sheet contains the assets (tangible and intangible items the business owns), liabilities (money the business owes) and equity which represent the investment that owners and partners use to fund the business. One of the major sources of equity for the business is the result of how well the operation is managed. If the business is managed well, a profit will be generated and that profit will be added each year to increase the equity on the balance sheet. A loss on the income statement reduces the equity on the balance sheet.

Chapter 10 – Financial Projections

Figure 15 – Example Balance Sheet ASB

ASB Company INC
Balance Sheet
December 31, 20XX
($ in thousands)

Assets
Current Assets
- Cash — 5000
- Accounts Recievable — 2000
- Inventory — 400
- Prepaid Insurance — 500
- Total Current Assets — 7900

Fixed Assets
- Equipment — 1000
- Property — 3000
- Less: Accumulated Depreciation — -600
- Total Fixed Assets less depreciation — 3400
- Total Assets — 11300

Liabilities and Owners Equity
Liabilities
- Accounts Payable — 4300
- Taxes Payable — 2000
- Long term Debt — 1000
- Total Liabilities — 7300

Owners Equity:
- Stocks or Invested Capital — 3000
- Retained Earnings — 1000
- Total Equity — 4000

Total Liabilities and Owners Equity — 11300

Chapter 10 – Financial Projections

Another significant area to take into consideration is cash flow. As a business owner, you want to ensure that you have sufficient cash on hand to meet your financial obligations. The three areas of cash flow include funds from resulting operations, investing and financing. For cash flow from operations, you should pay attention to monies (a) from the operations in terms of net profit, (b) customers owe to the business, called accounts receivable, (c) the level of goods on hand, called inventory and (d) what the business owes to suppliers and vendors, called accounts payable. The takeaway here is to remember that when you first start your business you must be aware of the uses and sources of cash.

If you are new at working with financials it is best to get help from a financial expert and to speak with your accountant.

<u>Key Points From This Chapter</u>

- Identify products and services pricing.
- What is the expected revenue on a weekly, monthly and yearly basis?
- What are your expected expenses on a weekly, monthly and yearly basis?
- Develop projected income statements, balance sheet and cash flow statements.
- Scale up business only after meeting key criteria.

Chapter 10 – Financial Projections

Learnings to Take Away 10

Why is it important to understand pricing of your products/services?

List any costs you will minimize by being competitive.

Chapter 10 – Financial Projections

What new financial concepts have you learned in this chapter?

What new financial topics could help your business?

Conclusion

Concluding Statement

The business plan is an essential road map for defining those key objectives that you want to complete in your business. I hope this book gave you some ideas about what you need to do to clearly communicate why you believe your business will be successful.

I appreciate you taking the time to read through this guide. It is my desire to inspire you to complete your business plan and use it to set goals that will help you advance your business and remain or become profitable.

If you need additional help in preparing your business plan, our company offers fee-based services for the facilitation of and advisory support for:

- Mission and Vision
- Business Plan
- Business Strategy
- Organizational Leadership Techniques
- Budgeting
- Financial Plan
- Product Pricing
- Business Finance Training for Leaders

Contact us at:
Zing4Success Strategic Management & Planning
Website address: https://zing4success.com/contact

Ideas and Notes

Ideas and Notes

ENTREPRENEUR'S ROAD MAP

Ideas and Notes

www.ingramcontent.com/pod-product-compliance
Lightning Source LLC
Chambersburg PA
CBHW050323010526
44119CB00003B/87